not a guide to
Cheltenham

Tom Lowe

The author wishes to express his appreciation to Camilla Bassett-Smith and David Singer for their kind assistance in creating this book, and would also like to thank all image contributors.

First published in 2012

The History Press
The Mill, Brimscombe Port
Stroud, Gloucestershire, GL5 2QG
www.thehistorypress.co.uk

British Library Cataloguing in Publication Data.
A catalogue record for this book is available from the British Library.

ISBN 978 0 7524 6883 9

Typesetting and origination by The History Press
Printed in Great Britain

The three birds, or pigeons, one at the top of the crest and two on the shield, symbolise the discovery of the town's famous spa waters – a flock of pigeons seen pecking at the salt deposited by an emerging mineral spring bestowed a lasting legacy. The colour blue also represents the hearty spa waters.

At the top of the shield are two books, typifying a place of educational excellence after the foundation of the Cheltenham Ladies' College and Cheltenham College.

Between the two books lies a white cross – that of Edward the Confessor, formerly Lord of the Manor of Cheltenham.

The oak tree on the shield and branches on the crest exemplify the many tree-lined thoroughfares that give the town a sense of grandeur.

The words *Salubritas et Eruditio* represent Cheltenham's motto, and translate into English as 'Health and Learning' – introducing the ancestry of its spa waters, and the town's reputation for academic eminence.

Contents

Definition of the Name

Pronounced: Chelt'nəm (ə pronounced like the 'e' in item), or 'tʃeltnəm using the International Phonetic Alphabet.

Originally named as *Celtanhomme*, or *Celtanham*, at the start of the ninth century. The first part of the name is possibly an Old English reference to the River Chelt that runs through the town, or a derivation of *Celta*, ancient British (pre-Roman) for hill or hill-slope. The latter part, *homme*, alluding to an enclosure or meadow beside a river or *ham*, meaning village or homestead.

Appearing in the Domesday Book in 1086 as the adapted *Chinteneham*, other variations of this were also recorded later. The present-day term was well established by the fourteenth century.

Grid Reference

'Centre Stone' – SO 94880 22584

The 'Centre Stone' is found embedded into the corner brickwork of the first floor of the jewellers F. Hinds' building, located on the corner of Bennington Street and the lower High Street. It is considered to be the exact centre of Cheltenham and is used as a focal point from where distances of other locations are determined.

Street Names

Promenade – You might think of finding one of these at the seaside, but the 'Prom' that runs in front of the Borough Council's Municipal Offices is arguably Cheltenham's finest thoroughfare.

Princess Elizabeth Way – The main arterial road running through Hester's Way. Built between 1951 and 1957, and named after Princess Elizabeth less than a year before her accession to the throne. Elizabeth paid a visit to the area to open the newly constructed Hester's Way estate with the planting of a solitary oak tree.

Normal Terrace – Quite normal! A thoroughfare that roughly joins the entrance to the Francis Close Hall campus of the University of Gloucestershire with the High Street, where it narrows to a tiny passageway. Named after a previous title for the campus, the Normal College, which was a teacher-training facility run by the Church of England.

Kidnappers Lane – Many rumours surround the naming. Some say it followed an actual kidnapping, others think that it points to 'press gangs' who would prowl the area, forcibly enlisting suitable men into the navy.

Arkle Close – Arkle, the Irish racehorse, was the unbeatable force in the Gold Cup in 1960s, winning three consecutive victories from 1964.

Imjin Road – Named in honour of the valiant efforts of the Gloucestershire Regiment, the 'Glorious Glosters', at the Battle of the Imjin River in 1951.

Districts

Battledown – The Battledown Estate dominates the area, and is one of the most affluent parts of the town.

Benhall – The Government Communications Headquarters, GCHQ, is based here.

Charlton Kings – Gives the first taste of Cheltenham to travellers along the A40 from London.

Hester's Way – Created to provide homes for GCHQ workers. It has since entered a period of regeneration, with new dwellings replacing high-rise tower blocks.

Leckhampton – Sits at the base of the majestic Leckhampton Hill.

Montpellier – Showcases fashionable boutiques, cafés and bars.

Pittville – Developed by Joseph Pitt in the nineteenth century, and includes the Pittville Pump Room, an impressive spa building.

Prestbury – Cheltenham Racecourse at Prestbury Park is found here. It also lays claim to being one of the most haunted parts of England.

St Paul's – Hosts the Francis Close Hall, a campus of the University of Gloucestershire, and possesses a large student population.

Whaddon – The home of Cheltenham Town Football Club.

BATTLEDOWN ESTATE
PRIVATE ROADS
NO
THROUGH TRAFFIC

VISITORS
ACCESS TO
BATTLEDOWN
ESTATE
VIA
HALES ROAD
AND
BATTLEDOWN
APPROACH

Distance from...

	Miles	Km
Ayres Rock (Uluru), Australia	9,399	15,127
Brussels, Belgium	287	462
Centre of the Earth	3,960	6,371
Death Valley, USA	5,185	8,344
Eiffel Tower, Paris	285	459
Frankfurt, Germany	484	778
Glasgow, Scotland	288	463
Hong Kong, China	6,043	9,725
Istanbul, Turkey	1,643	2,645
Jerusalem, Israel	2,333	3,755
The Kremlin, Russia	1,619	2,606
Lima, Peru	6,255	10,067
The Moon (average distance)	238,857	384,403
Niagara Falls, North America	3,479	5,599
Osaka, Japan	5,934	9,549
Panama Canal, Republic of Panama	5,198	8,365
Queenstown, New Zealand	11,814	19,013
Reykjavik, Iceland	1,107	1,782
Syracuse, Sicily	1,330	2,141
The Taj Mahal, India	4,359	7,016
Ural Mountains, Russia	2,310	3,717
Vatican City	971	1,563
Washington DC, USA	3,580	5,762
Xanthi, Greece	1,471	2,367
Yellowstone National Park, USA	4,553	7,327
Zurich, Switzerland	569	915

How Far from the 'Centre Stone'?

	Minutes	Miles
Everyman Theatre	4	0.21
Town Hall	8	0.41
Cheltenham Ladies' College	9	0.47
Montpellier Gardens	10	0.52
Cheltenham Town Football Club	15	0.78
Cheltenham College	17	0.86
Pittville Pump Room	18	0.94
Cheltenham Racecourse	24	1.22
Cheltenham Spa railway station	27	1.37
GCHQ	46	2.39

Twin Towns

Annecy, France – While Cheltenham is famed for its mineral springs and the surrounding Cotswold Hills, Annecy lays claim to the pure water of Lake Annecy, which it perches beside, and the encircling Alps. The two localities forged a special partnership in 1956.

Cheltenham, Pennsylvania, USA – Linked in 1950, after the presentation of a silver platter to the Township from the then Mayor of Cheltenham. It seems logical that there be a tie – not only do they share the same name, but the same crest and motto, 'Health and Learning'.

Göttingen, Germany – A very special bond has been forged between the towns ever since the twinning link was made in 1951, particularly through the annual 'Festivals' or 'Big Party' visits that are hosted for large groups of people travelling between the two towns every year.

Sochi, Russia – Recommended by the Soviet Embassy as an obvious partner, as Sochi is also a spa town – it bears the Matsesta ('fire water') Spa, the famous local hot sulphur springs. One intriguing way that Sochi connects with Cheltenham, and the rest of the world, is through its citrus 'Tree of Friendship', which has grown from buds grafted to it by visitors.

Weihai, China – A former British colony, the first links were made in the 1980s, with official twinning status granted in 1998. Weihai also complements Cheltenham with many natural hot springs sprinkled throughout the city.

Friendship Towns:
Kisumu, Kenya and Stampersgat, the Netherlands.

Other Cheltenhams

Cheltenham, Auckland, New Zealand

Cheltenham, Maryland, USA

Cheltenham, New South Wales, Australia

Cheltenham, Pennsylvania, USA

Cheltenham, St Louis, Missouri, USA

Cheltenham, South Australia, Australia

Cheltenham, Victoria, Australia

Cheltenham Badlands, Caledon, Ontario, Canada

Timeline

Pate's Grammar School, the first school in the town, opens.

The first post office opens at No. 127 High Street.

St Mary's parish church built.

Discovery of mineral springs establishes Cheltenham as a spa town.

On 4 June, the Cheltenham and Gloucester Tramroad publicly opens.

c.1011　　**1574**　　　**1716**　　　**1800**　　　**1811**

1226　　**1628**　　　**1788**　　　**1809**　　　**1823**

King Henry III of England grants the town a market charter.

On 12 July, an ailing King George III visits Cheltenham to indulge in the healing spa waters.

The iconic Cavendish House department store is established.

Manor of Cheltenham purchased from the Prince of Wales, Charles I, by John Dutton Esq. of Sherborne for £1,200.

On 4 May, the *Cheltenham Chronicle* was established as the first local newspaper.

On 3 October, John Hampton performs an early parachute jump, ascending via hot-air balloon from Montpellier Gardens.

On 5 December, the Town Hall opens.

In May, the Regent Arcade opens on the former site of the Plough Hotel at a cost of £23 million.

Pittville Pump Room opens. It cost £60,000 to build.

The Cheltenham Ladies' College is founded.

1830　**1838**　　**1853**　　**1903**　　　　**1985**

1825　**1838**　　**1840**　　**1902**　　**1951**

On 21 July, The Queens Hotel opens.

Cheltenham Racecourse hosts the first Cheltenham Festival at Prestbury Park.

Local entrepreneur Joseph Pitt creates the Pittville estate.

Mainline rail transport arrives with the opening of Lansdown railway station.

GCHQ moves to Benhall and Oakley.

Freak Weather

January 1634 – Cheltenham is overwhelmed by a snowstorm for three weeks. Fierce gusts of wind damage housing and many residents die while out travelling on roads in the area.

27 November 1703 – A great storm severely damages St Mary's parish church and many houses.

5 June 1731 – Damage to the town amounting to £2,000 is caused by an intense hailstorm.

26 December 1860 – A frost occurs so severe that a cricket match is able to take place on the iced-over Pittville Lake.

January 1881 – A harsh blizzard brings 7in of snow to Cheltenham, drifting as much as 7ft in places. A bone-chilling temperature of -19.4°C (-2.9°F) is recorded on the 20th.

December 1962 to March 1963 – Heavy snow and bitterly cold winds paralyse much of the town. Cheltenham Racecourse is kept operational for the National Hunt Festival by teams of groundspeople clearing snow by hand to preserve the turf.

3 July 1976 – The hottest day of the hottest UK summer, at that point, since records began is recorded in Cheltenham, with a temperature of 35.9°C (96.6°F)

25 January 1990 – Hurricane-force winds batter the town, which suffers more than during the Great Storm of 1987. A horse chestnut tree falls opposite Neptune's Fountain on the Promenade and fatally wounds the female driver of a soft-top car.

3 August 1990 – Cheltenham claims the national record for highest recorded temperature when Montpellier Gardens bakes in the heat of 37.1°C (98.8°F).

20 July 2007 – Rainfall of biblical proportions brings devastating flooding to Cheltenham. Three months' worth of rain falls in just thirty-four hours, and the River Chelt bursts its banks. Blue bowsers appear on every street corner as clean drinking water dries up.

A Day in the Life

Sleepy-eyed commuters await the first train to London Paddington at Cheltenham Spa.

The Wishing Fish Clock in the Regent Arcade Shopping Centre entertains its first visitors, with a large wooden fish beginning its half-hourly celebration of spouting bubbles to onlookers.

The first Arle Court Park & Ride bus arrives on the 'Prom'.

Viewings underway around Cheltenham Animal Shelter.

0545   **0730**   **0900**   **1200**

0630   **0850**   **1130**

Early risers hit the treadmills at leisure@cheltenham.

Saturday walking tours start at the Tourist Information Centre.

Lessons commence at the Cheltenham Ladies' College.

Evening drinks
poured at Montpellier
Wine Bar.

Final hour of
Cheltenham's Friday
Farmers' Market on
the 'Prom'.

Curtain up at the
Everyman Theatre.

1400   **1830**   **1945**

1230   **1500**   **1930**   **2300**

Pittville Lake comes alive
with aspiring seafarers.

Weekend revellers
join the party at
Subtone nightclub.

Lunchtime prayers begin
in Cheltenham's oldest
building, St Mary's parish
church.

Dinner is served at
the two-star Michelin
restaurant Le Champignon
Sauvage.

How Many Times a Year...

...do major race meetings take place at Cheltenham Racecourse?

8

...are the town centre streets cleaned?

1,095

...does the Cheltenham Farmers' Market display its wares on the 'Prom'?

26

...do Cheltenham Town Football Club play League games at Whaddon Road?

23

...are individual plants bedded into display areas around town?

25,000

...does the cultural organisation Cheltenham Festivals deliver entertainment?

4

...do the Cheltenham Operatic and Dramatic Society produce shows?

3

...are tickets purchased for Cheltenham 'Big Four' Festivals?

Over 150,000

...does Cheltenham host the German Christmas Market?

17

Demographics

(Source: 2001 Census, ONS)

Population:

Total:	110,013	
Men:	53,379	(48.52 per cent)
Women:	56,634	(51.48 per cent)

Age:

Fifteen and under:	20,207	(18.37 per cent)
Between sixteen and seventy-four:	79,804	(72.54 per cent)
Seventy-five and over:	10,002	(9.09 per cent)

Marital status (all people aged over sixteen):

Single (never married):	30,633	(34.11 per cent)
Married or re-married:	41,873	(46.63 per cent)
Separated or divorced:	9,699	(10.80 per cent)
Widowed:	7,601	(8.46 per cent)

Ethnicity:

White:	106,335	(96.66 per cent)
Largest Minority Ethnic Group –		
Indian:	1,095	(1.00 per cent)
Largest Religion – Christian:	79,581	(72.34 per cent)

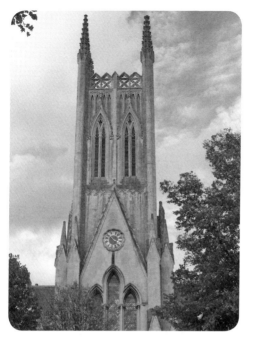

Strange Statistics

1 – Position achieved by Cheltenham, out of a list of 1,833 areas of England, in a list of 'desirable places within which to own property', compiled by propertypriceadvice.co.uk in 2006.

2 – Amount of Cheltenham neighbourhoods that are within the most deprived 10 per cent in England.

26 – Square kilometres of land covered by the Borough of Cheltenham.

80 – Percent of visitors to the Cheltenham Science Festival who reside in the immediately surrounding postcodes.

81.7 – Miles per hour achieved by the London-bound 'Cheltenham Flyer' passenger-train service between Swindon and London Paddington on Monday, 6 June 1932, thus becoming the world's fastest steam train.

108.4 – Decibels generated by the 'Cheltenham roar' of the jubilant crowd at the start of the first race of the 2010 Cheltenham Festival.

287 – Length, in feet, of the façade of the Cavendish House department store.

326 – Years, in total, that the Plough Hotel in Cheltenham spent welcoming guests. It was demolished to make way for the Regent Arcade Shopping Centre.

600 – Properties in Cheltenham that have a 1 per cent annual chance of flooding.

1864 – Year the first burial was performed at Cheltenham Cemetery.

6,212 – Total distance, in yards, of the long holes at Lilley Brook Golf Club.

9,615 – Pounds charged to send one student to board, per term, at the Cheltenham Ladies' College (as at September 2011).

15,700 – Pounds spent on the construction of Sandford Parks Lido by its completion in 1935.

Literary Quotations

'Cheltenham is a nasty, ill-looking place, half clown and half cockney. The town is one street about a mile long; but, then, at some distance from this street, there are rows of white tenements, with green balconies, like those inhabited by the tax-eaters round London. Indeed, this place appears to be the residence of an assemblage of tax-eaters.'

William Cobbett, *Rural Rides*, 1830

'While the Arden family are on their way to town, we shall take a peep at the High-street in Cheltenham. Strings of carriages were driving backward and forward, from turnpike to turnpike, while the open barouches, filled with bonnets of every colour in the rainbow, flaunting and waving to and fro, looked like so many moving beds of full-blown tulips. Foot-passengers too of all classes thronged the flagways.'

Margratia Loudon, *Dilemmas of Pride, by the Author of First Love*, 1833

'The shop lights threw their red glare over the snow-bedded ground as we entered the town of Cheltenham, and nothing but the drift and ourselves moved through the deserted streets. ... Cheltenham is a fashionable town, a watering, visiting place, where everything is genteel and thin.'

George Jacob Holyoake, *The History of the Last Trial by Jury for Atheism In England*, 1851

'Here lies I and my three daughters,

Killed by a drinking the Cheltenham waters;

If we had stuck to Epsom salts,

We'd not been a lying in these here vaults.'

Horatio Edward Norfolk, *Gleanings In Graveyards*, 1861

'The *elité* of at least half the shire is present, and Miss Linton, who is still the hostess, reigns supreme in fine exuberance of spirits ... on this night present she lives as in the past; almost fancies herself back at Cheltenham in its days of splendour, and dancing with "the first gentleman in Europe" redivivus.'

Captain Mayne Reid, *Gwen Wynn: A Romance of the Wye*, 1877

'They entered Cheltenham at about half-past eleven, and were having lunch on top of Leckhampton Hill, on the other side of it, by half-past one. Robert had not allowed any stop in Cheltenham except for shopping. "We don't want towns," he said, "except historic ones." "But this is historic," said Jack; "Jessop was at school here."'

E.V. Lucas, *The Slowcoach*, 1910

'For the chimney-sweeps of Cheltenham town,

Sooty of face as a swallow of wing,

Come whistling, singing, dancing down

With white teeth flashing as they sing.'

Alfred Noyes, *The New Morning: Poems*, 1918

Famous Homes

Fred Archer, the famous jockey – St George's Cottage, St George's Place.

Sir Benjamin Baker, civil engineer – 'Farm Cottage', on the site of No. 4 Cambray Place.

Sir Arthur T. Harris, Marshal of the RAF, BT. GCB, OBE, AFC, LLD. Chief of Bomber Command during the Second World War – 3 Queen's Parade.

Gustav Holst, composer – 4 Clarence Road (was Pittville Terrace).

Dr Edward Jenner, discoverer of vaccination – Alpha House, St George's Road.

Brian Jones, founder of the Rolling Stones – 'Rosemead', 17 Eldorado Road.

William Charles Macready, actor – 6 Wellington Square.

John Nevil Maskelyne, illusionist and watchmaker – 12 Rotunda Terrace, Montpellier.

Sir Frederick Handley Page, aviation pioneer – 3 Kings Road.

Sir Thomas Phillipps, antiquarian and book collector – Thirlestaine Hall, Thirlestaine Road.

Sir Ralph Richardson, actor – 11 Tivoli Road.

Sir Robert Smirke, architect – Montpellier House, Suffolk Square.

Charles Sturt, Australian explorer – 19 Clarence Square.

Alfred, Lord Tennyson, Poet Laureate – 10 St James' Square.

Edward Wilson, explorer – 91 Montpellier Terrace.

Sir Norman Wisdom, O.B.E., comedian, actor, singer – Hotel du Vin (formerly Carlton Hotel), Parabola Road.

Famous for...

Regency Architecture – Particularly evident in the Municipal Offices, the home of Cheltenham Borough Council that faces the Promenade; The Queens Hotel, perched on the corner of Imperial Gardens; and the terraces of Lansdown Crescent and Montpellier Spa Road. The town has been referred to as the most complete Regency town in England.

The Cheltenham Gold Cup – The crown jewel of all National Hunt racing, it takes place on the final day of the Cheltenham Festival every year in March. It has previously been won by great names such as Best Mate, Arkle and Golden Miller. The cup itself is made of nine-carat solid gold.

Gustav Holst – The revered English composer most famous for creating *The Planets* orchestral suite. The Holst Birthplace Museum in the town was opened in his memory, and there is a statue dedicated to him in Imperial Gardens.

GCHQ (The Government Communication Headquarters) – The intelligence agency that operates alongside the Security Service (MI5) and the Secret Intelligence Service (MI6) protecting the security interests of the UK.

Festivals – Showcased at many venues in the town, but centred mainly around the Town Hall, these festivals have built an enviable international reputation. The 'Big Four' are the Jazz, Science, Music and Literature Festivals.

The Cheltenham Ladies' College – The educational establishment that remains extremely prominent all over the world as a centre for high-quality schooling.

Infamous for...

The inner ring road – Notoriously complex to visitors, and the source of much debate over the years. The fingers point to excessive amounts of traffic lights, poor signage, and the troublesome bottlenecks of Clarence Street and North Street, which often get crowded with parked buses. Cheltenham Borough Council has made many attempts to improve and regenerate it since the one-way system was introduced in 1971.

The 'Second-Last' on the Old Course – The obstacle at Cheltenham Racecourse, called 'one of the toughest fences in jump racing', which has caused numerous horses to fall and has claimed several lives. It has now been repositioned on the home straight and away from the final turn.

Making the Headlines

26 January 1984

'The government faced an immense backlash last night over its decision to ban workers at the Government Communications Headquarters in Cheltenham from being part of a trade union and from taking any strike action. There is an offer of £1,000 compensation from Westminster for any loss of statutory rights. Fears are already growing of mass protests to the arrangement. The TUC has said it is in full support of the Civil Service unions in fighting the ban.'

16 July 1982

'A major spy scandal has developed as Cheltenham taxi driver Geoffrey Prime is charged under the Official Secrets Act with unspecified acts of espionage after his infiltration of computer-stored secrets at GCHQ. Press reports said he had worked at GCHQ from 1968 to 1978, and the charges only suggested that the acts had been going on for fourteen years.'

December 1860

'With a row of trees being planted either side of the Lansdown Road, the first planted in a special ceremony on the 14th, the *Cheltenham Examiner* states that once the trees have attained a few weeks growth, it will be, without doubt, one of the finest drives in the kingdom. It will form, in fact, the Champs Élysées of Cheltenham.'

1788

'As King George III, Queen Charlotte and the Royal Princesses visited Cheltenham, the *Morning Post* reports that "in consequence of the overflow of Cheltenham, Tewkesbury and Prestbury are crowded... Cheltenham will be the summer village of all that is fashionable – the Cheltenham bonnets, Cheltenham buttons and Cheltenham buckles being quite the go – the fashions being completely Cheltenhamized throughout the kingdom".'

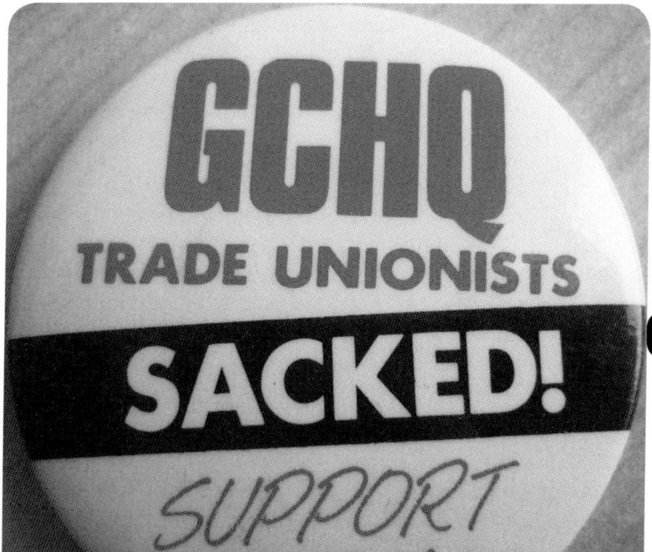
GCHQ
TRADE UNIONISTS
SACKED!
SUPPORT
THEM

Letters to the Press

'Seagull Cull'

One solution to attempt to control the increasing numbers of gulls in Cheltenham in 2010 was to shoot them, suggested at a public meeting at the council's Municipal Offices and reaffirmed by the council's environmental protection department.

One commented on hellish nights on the Kingsditch Trading Estate because of the birds, which made a dreadful racket from 4 a.m. every morning. It wasn't discarded food that was attracting them, but the many tall buildings, which they used as prime nesting sites. Something had to be done, and shooting the birds was one way to do it, just to get some peace and quiet.

Another countered by saying that culling by the gun would just cause a temporary decline in numbers, providing empty nesting sites and extra food for other gulls, which would then breed in healthier and more comfortable conditions. The solution to this problem was to eliminate any nesting sites and reduce the supply of food.

'This is a Sign!'

Paddy Power, the owner of Ireland's largest bookmaker, erected the world's longest freestanding sign, spelling out his very name on the side of Cleeve Hill, overlooking the Cheltenham Festival at Cheltenham Racecourse in 2010.

Locals certainly had a difference of opinion. One guarded against adding coloured flashing lights around the edge, as it would bring Cheltenham closer to looking 'as tacky as Las Vegas'. Another wanted the sign to be made bigger so he could see it from his house outside the town. A third questioned planning permission.

Other thoughts ranged from it being 'a bit of fun' to boycotting the bookmaker until it was taken down.

'Disrespectful Disruption?'

A clothing store on the Promenade switched on its sound system and played loud pop music during Cheltenham's Remembrance Day Parade in 2009.

Cheltonians were outraged. Comments ranged from 'appalling' to 'shocked' and 'disgusted'. One lady even told of a request by her parents to boycott the store. But another offered some contemplative reflection, mentioning the staff in store that would have been following silly rigid rules imposed by head office management to follow store presentation guidelines to the letter.

'Another Fine Mess'

Cheltenham pedestrians had to watch their step in 2007 after the local council gave an order to street cleaners to leave dog mess un-cleared. Dog wardens were to be called instead to paint colour coded rings around the deposit to highlight the problem to the canine owners.

A resident voiced his concern about the problem, but thought this idea was too batty, especially with odour issues in hot weather. Potential risks to health were highlighted by some, as was the visual aspects of the marked pavements, which would resemble a bizarre piece of modern art!

Rebellious Cheltenham

Fathers 4 Justice
Two Cheltenham men, campaigning for the group Fathers 4 Justice, attempted to scale the walls of Buckingham Palace dressed as Batman and Robin on 13 September 2004. 'Batman' succeeded, and staged a protest from a ledge next to the palace's main balcony about fathers' rights of access to their children after a separation. A banner was unfurled reading, 'Super Dads of Fathers 4 Justice', and 'Fighting for your rights to kids', before the caped crusader was apprehended via a crane.

Insurgent Investors
Members of the Cheltenham & Gloucester Building Society filled Cheltenham Town Hall on 25 March 1995 to protest against its takeover by Lloyds. C&G directors were heckled for two hours as investors challenged the lack of cash bonuses to the owners of accounts held for less than two years.

Poll Tax
Forty-eight people were arrested, and two police officers were hurt, as protestors, revolting against the introduction of the Poll Tax, hurled rocks and other debris at the security cordon put up outside Cheltenham Town Hall on 31 March 1990. Prime Minster Margaret Thatcher was addressing the Conservative Party Central Council meeting inside.

Buildings & Architecture

Most Desirable

Surely the Council's Municipal Offices, on the 'Prom', are the most prime piece of property in all of Cheltenham. George Allen Underwood designed the impressive terrace in 1825. Originally intended for private residences, it was known as 'Harward's Buildings', after Samuel Harward (who had a large hand in developing the Promenade). The building became the Municipal Offices in 1915, with Cheltenham Borough Council occupying the majority by the late 1950s. Suggestions of the council relinquishing the buildings for leisure use have been made regularly.

Biggest Eyesore

The Quadrangle in Cheltenham has a tough reputation to keep up with. After all, its bleak mix of grey brick and uninspiring glass struggles to match the splendour of its Regency neighbours. Built in 1973 on the site of a Victorian members' club, it was originally revered as a visionary modern design. In recent times it has deteriorated somewhat, and has spent a substantial period hidden by metal scaffolding.

Oldest

St Mary's parish church, situated just to the south of the lower High Street, dates from Norman times and has an entry in the Domesday Book. It is said to have been built on the old foundations of a monastery from around the eighth century. The piers supporting the tower arches and the nave's west wall are the oldest parts, with further construction apparent in the latter part of the thirteenth century.

Tallest

Eagle Tower (formerly the Eagle Star Building, home to Eagle Star Insurance) opened in 1968 and stands 161ft high. When the building changed hands in 2003, rumours circulated of a possible redevelopment of the upper floors into residential accommodation, with a panoramic restaurant, but nothing further arose. The bird's eye view of Cheltenham from the roof is breathtaking.

Most Extraordinary

The 'Doughnut', the name that Cheltonians affectionately use to refer to the home of GCHQ, is an outstanding feat of engineering. The building was designed by British architect Chris Johnson and took three years to build at a cost of £337 million. It stands 70ft tall, 600ft in diameter and covers an area of 176 acres. From the outside the construction is a mixture of overwhelming glass and rigid metal, but local Cotswold stone is also incorporated. The courtyard in the centre is large enough for the Royal Albert Hall to fit in the middle. It was officially opened by the Queen in March 2004.

Most Controversial

To place the radical looking Millennium Restaurant, built on the corner of Portland Street and Fairview Road, in amongst the fine Regency buildings of Cheltenham was always going to be difficult task to achieve! Built in 1997 at a staggering cost of £1.5 million, the space-age style design didn't win many friends, especially its bizarre roof construction. It soon closed, only to become home to a health and fitness club, then lay derelict until 2005, when it was demolished. A luxury apartment building was erected in its place.

Most Lifelike

The buildings of Montpellier Walk are supported by a collective of elegant women... literally! Standing proud between each dwelling, some grouping to brace individual establishments, are thirty-three white caryatids – sculpted female figures, heads erect and draped in flowing dresses, carrying the majesty of the brasseries and boutiques on their heads, taking inspiration from similar statues underpinning the roof of the Acropolis in Greece. The statues, all of them in position by the mid-nineteenth century, were carved from stone by W.G. Brown from the Tivoli area of town, with only some originals, from 1843, produced from terracotta and created by the English sculptor John Charles Felix Rossi.

Museums

Cheltenham Art Gallery & Museum

This opened in 1899, after acquiring several paintings from town mayor and MP Baron Charles de Ferrieres, who donated £1,000 to create the gallery where they could be displayed. The museum's collections include many displays on local history. There is a section devoted to local Antarctic explorer Edward Wilson, featuring an array of his expedition possessions, and a nationally-important collection on the Arts & Crafts Movement in Britain, held by the museum since the 1930s, including works by Charles Robert Ashbee and the Guild of Handicraft at Chipping Campden.

Significant improvements to visitor facilities came in 1989, when HRH The Princess Royal opened an extension to the building. In 2011, the museum closed temporarily to undergo a redevelopment programme costing £6.3 million.

Holst Birthplace Museum

Occupies the Regency terraced house, on No. 4 Pittville Terrace (now Clarence Road), where Gustav Holst was born in 1874 and where he spent his early years.

The museum was founded by his daughter Imogen and opened in 1975 in commemoration of Holst's life and works. As you explore the house you find some of Holst's furniture and personal belongings alongside works of art and photographs – but, as you enter, you almost immediately encounter the Music Room, which proudly displays the very piano on which Holst composed much of *The Planets* suite. The building is an enduring biography of Holst, of Victorian-Edwardian home living, and is one of only two museums in the country established at the birthplace of a composer; the other honours Edward Elgar.

Iconic Image

Parks

Sandford Park
Historically significant, with a reference in the Domesday Book, and once home to Cheltenham's former mills. The River Chelt is also clearly visible from here.

Pittville Park
Grade II listed, with Pittville Lake and Pump Room to boast to visitors.

Hatherley Park
A multiple winner of the Green Flag Awards, developed from land that was originally part of Hatherley Court Estate.

Hester's Way Park
The park has its own stone-circle monument, created through a public art project, featuring engraved text.

Naunton Park
Features a prominent 'Weeping Beech', with a row of cottage homes overlooking the ornamental area.

Springfields Park
A transformation from an intimidating vicinity to an aspiring community area has seen the addition of a resource centre and landscaping with wild flowers.

Green Spaces & Gardens

Long Gardens
Perched perfectly in front of the Municipal Offices – a splendid advertisement for Cheltenham's floral excellence.

Imperial Gardens
Once the exclusive domain of the visitors to Sherborne Spa, but now providing a nearby refuge from the town's bustle.

Montpellier Gardens
Displays a bandstand (one of the oldest in the country), the proscenium building as a cultural venue, and tennis courts.

Cox's Meadow
Originally hosted funfairs and events but now serves as a flood plain for the town, with an overflow gate for the River Chelt.

Queen Elizabeth Playing Fields
Based on the site of the Battledown Brick and Terracotta Co. clay pits that helped construct many of Cheltenham's buildings.

Jenner Gardens
The graveyard of the former Cheltenham Chapel, resting just a stone's throw from the Lower High Street.

Winston Churchill Memorial Garden
This hosts a Grade II listed chapel and a drinking fountain embossed with messages.

Local Flora & Fauna

Cheltenham in Bloom
The committee that actively promotes the town's floral heritage. Cheltenham has won the national 'In Bloom' competition on several occasions, and has also been the winner of the 'Prix European d'Excellence'.

Birds and Bunnies
An area of Pittville Park that is always popular with Cheltonians and visitors alike. It is exclusively tailored for an array of rabbits, chipmunks, peacocks, finches and other birds, and is maintained by the 'Support Our Birds and Bunnies Committee'.

Champion Trees
Three trees in Cheltenham have been commended in the Tree Register's Official Champion Tree Database, detailing notable and ancient trees: the 'Smooth Arizona Cypress' in front of the entrance to Cheltenham College; the 'St Lucie Cherry' on the north-east side of Hester's Way Park; and the 'Pencil Cedar' in Pittville Park, just south of the Pump Room.

Pigeons
If it hadn't have been for the famous flock nibbling at the salts from an emerging spring, then Cheltenham's future would have been vastly different. The initiators of the town's spa tradition are immortalised in the form of several small black metal statues a-top signposts throughout the town.

Elephants
Not strictly from Cheltenham, but they certainly caused a local stir in 1934 when three elephants, from Chapman's Great London Zoo and in town for a show, caused a stampede while parading along Albion Street. Two managed to break free from their reins and proceeded to help themselves to the wares of local pet shop Bloodworth's. The charade is portrayed in a collective of murals in an alleyway leading off the upper end of the pedestrianised High Street.

Businesses & Companies

GCHQ

The British intelligence agency relocated its operation from north-west London to Cheltenham in 1951, where it operated from two sites, one at Oakley and the other at Benhall. GCHQ employs around 5,500 people, and the majority are based at the 'Doughnut' at Benhall, where work involves providing information to the government to assist national security, defence and law enforcement policies, and protecting Government data from external sabotage.

Spirax Sarco

Manufacturers in steam and boiler technology, this is a multinational business that employs over 4,400 people worldwide – including more than 1,300 specialist engineers. Its head office is in Charlton House on Cirencester Road, with a manufacturing plant on the Kingsditch Trading Estate.

GE Aviation

The aerospace company that superseded two key Cheltenham names in aeronautical engineering: Smiths Aerospace and Dowty Group. In 2005, two years before the GE Aviation takeover, Smiths reported a £141 million turnover and employed over 900 people. Smiths acquired the TI Group at the turn of the twenty-first century – which, in turn, had owned the Dowty Group, the firm that originally started out as Dowty Aviation in a factory at Arle Court in 1935.

Kohler Mira Ltd

Best known for its flagship product, the Mira shower. The shower and bathroom fittings manufacturer established their manufacturing base in the town in 1937, and employs around 850 staff at its headquarters on Cromwell Road in Whaddon. They are currently the main shirt sponsors of Cheltenham Town Football Club.

Kraft Foods UK

Over 500 people worked at their UK and Ireland headquarters at St George's House on Bayshill Road, originally arriving in the town in the mid-1970s. The food-processing giant has previously sponsored 'Cheltenham in Bloom' and other events since being based in the town. Kraft's Cheltenham operations closed in 2011.

Chelsea Building Society

The building society's administrative headquarters have been based in Cheltenham since 1973, when Thirlestaine Hall was chosen as a home. Further expansion in the town occurred in 2006, when an environmentally friendly, purpose-built contact centre began operations on the site of the old Charlton Kings railway station. By the end of 2011, all Thirlestaine Hall staff had relocated to Charlton Kings.

UCAS

The Universities and Colleges Admissions Service for British students, which deals with more than 2 million full-time undergraduate course applications every year. UCAS is based on New Barn Lane, opposite Cheltenham Racecourse. In 2011, following the release of the latest A-Level results, the Service's website crashed after receiving 450 requests per second.

Nelson Thornes

Founded in 1968, first as Stanley Thornes and then, after it acquired Thomas Nelson & Sons, as Nelson Thornes. They are one of the leading educational publishing firms in the country, with their main office on Bath Road.

Political Figures

James Agg-Gardner
Part of the town's brewing dynasty, Gardner's, who were based in the town since 1760, then morphed into the Cheltenham Original Brewing Co., and traded under that name for seventy-five years. Agg-Gardner first held the Cheltenham seat as MP in 1874, and returned after being re-elected a further three times over the following forty years.

Charles de Ferrieres
Famous instigator of the town's art gallery, and long-time resident of Bayshill House (where George III stayed during his visit), de Ferrieres was Cheltenham's MP from 1880 to 1885. As a memoriam to him, several stained glass windows can be found at St Peter's church in Leckhampton, where he is also buried.

Douglas Dodds-Parker
MP for Cheltenham from 1964 to 1974. Dodds-Parker famously showed his discontent at British involvement in the invasion of Egypt during the Suez Crisis of 1956, while a junior Foreign Office minister, and was eventually dismissed by Harold Macmillan for his views.

Charles Irving
A popular figure, serving his constituents devotedly from 1974 to 1992. He introduced the Gloucestershire medals of courage, awarded regularly to the brave and courageous. Irving's ashes were scattered over the town from the air in 1995. The Charles Irving Charitable Trust, inaugurated in commemoration of his life, supports the elderly, the disabled and various local community projects.

In memory of the Baron Du Bois de Ferrieres the last of the family died 1908 aged 84

Scientific Discoveries

In the late eighteenth century, Cheltenham's reputation as a source of good health was advocated through its life-giving, newly discovered spa waters. But, nearby, another discovery was taking place that would also put the town on the map as a health pioneer: Dr Edward Jenner was embarking on the development of the smallpox vaccine, created from the pus of the cowpox blister and shown to render immunity to the deadly disease.

Much of the early discovery and evolution took place 20 miles away at Berkeley, but Jenner would devote much of his life to the continuing crusade in Cheltenham, at two sites: St George's Place, where he would live, and Alpha House, on St George's Road, where he would set up a clinic. Jenner would visit a cabin on Cleeve Hill, overlooking Cheltenham, where he would source the vaccine from the grazing cows. Much of the development of the mixture would take place at St George's Place, where it would be distributed around the country (and overseas), and the administration of the vaccine would occur at Alpha House. It was free to the poor and the needy, such was Jenner's generosity, and queues of people, hundreds at a time, awaited their experience of the newly discovered life-saving drug.

Cheltenham was in the middle of a salubrious revolution: the road in which Jenner lived was filled with physicians and practitioners, all of whom were keen to embrace the vaccination advancement. In time, many colleagues and friends would visit Cheltenham to learn more from Jenner about his revolutionary practices.

The Cow Pock — or — the Wonderful Effects of the New Inoculation! — Vide. the Publications of ye Anti-Vaccine Society

Local Characters

'Dancing' Ken Hanks

Ken is a town legend. He was a local candidate for the Official Monster Raving Loony Party before stepping down from politics in 2010, after thirteen years' service. 'Dancing Ken' lives in a colourfully illustrated end-of-terrace house in Waterloo Place. One of his most famous policies advocated free motorised shoes for the elderly. He is also much-loved for his ongoing charity work, which has raised more than £1 million. He currently runs a Country and Western dance evening in Gloucester.

Ken Brightwell

Cheltenham's long-serving town crier, instilled in 1991, is a regular master-of-ceremonies at events all over town. They include the announcement of the latest crime figures on the 'Prom', giving a warm welcome to the 'In Bloom' judges in Imperial Gardens, and giving talks to local clubs and schools. Ken lives in Charlton Kings.

Crimes & Mysteries

The Torso Murder

In one of the most mysterious murders in British history, a body – believed to be that of Captain William Butt of No. 248 Old Bath Road, Leckhampton, who had been missing for weeks – was found in the River Severn near Haw Bridge, Tewkesbury. It was discovered on 3 February 1938. Dismembered limbs were additionally recovered, but the head and hands were missing.

Reports of a homosexual relationship involving one Brian Sullivan circulated. Sullivan was later found, dead, at Tower Lodge on Leckhampton Hill; apparently he had committed suicide. A blood-stained coat was discovered underneath the floorboards. Despite an extensive investigation, the jury at the inquest in Cheltenham returned an open verdict, as they had insufficient evidence to make any other ruling. The case remains unsolved.

Samurai Attack

A Liberal Democrat politician was seriously injured after a vicious sword attack which saw his colleague and close friend fatally wounded on 28 January 2000. MP for Cheltenham Nigel Jones recovered in hospital after fighting off an assault from the attacker at the party office in St George's Street, Cheltenham. Liberal Democrat councillor Andrew Pennington was killed as he attempted to defend Mr Jones.

The Baby Butcher

In 1896, Plough Hotel barmaid Evelina Marmon placed a newspaper advertisement requesting offers for the adoption of her illegitimate daughter. Next to Marmon's plea was another, a proposal to foster healthy children into a 'nice country home'. It had been placed by 'Mrs Harding' – an alias of prolific baby-farm murderer Amelia Dyer. The two made contact, the new-born was handed over to 'Harding', and Marmon bid a tearful farewell to her daughter at Cheltenham's Lansdown railway station. The infant was brutally murdered before being disposed of in a weir. Dyer was eventually arrested, tried and hanged at London's Newgate prison.

Ghosts

Prestbury's Phantoms

Prestbury is reputedly one of the most haunted parts of Great Britain:

The infamous apparition of the **Black Abbot** is legendary – originally frequenting the aisle through Prestbury's St Mary's church, before an exorcism was performed; then the churchyard, and Reform Cottage, especially the front garden, once a monk's burial ground. The disturbances occur mainly on days of holy commemoration: Easter, All Saints' Day and Christmas.

A **Headless Horseman** is rumoured to roam the streets. Legend has it that the ghost is the legacy of a messenger on horseback who was journeying from Sudeley Castle, a few miles north, through the village to Gloucester, during the Civil War, when he was decapitated by a thin piece of wire strung along the byway by the Roundheads of Prestbury.

In the grounds of the Prestbury House Hotel, in The Burgage, the **ghost of a young girl** is said to wander; the **sound of spectral horses' hooves** has also been reported. Rumours also circulate that the middle front window of the top floor of the hotel has been boarded up in the past because of sightings of the girl staring through the glass pane.

Sundial Cottage, also in The Burgage, holds the **spirit of another young girl**, this time seen to be playing a spinet – although latterly only the sounds of the instrument have been reported.

Numerous other ghosts have been seen, and heard, including the **funeral cortège** seen in a field near the junction of Southam Road and Mill Lane, **apparitions** and **poltergeists** in Idsall House, and **various miscellaneous sightings** inside – and outside – homes and businesses along the High Street.

The Cheltenham Ghost

Said to be of a tall woman, dressed in black, and holding a handkerchief to her face with her right hand as if inconsolably crying, this woman is believed to have haunted 'St Anne's', a house on Pittville Circus Road built by Henry Swinhoe in 1860.

The house itself was the home of the Despard family, and it was young Rosina, daughter of Captain Frederick Despard, who accounted for many of the several encounters with the spectre that were reported during the 1880s. The figure was apparently that of Mrs Imogen Swinhoe, the second wife of Henry Swinhoe; in life, she had struggled to deal with her husband's alcoholism. Encounters with the ghost began again seventy years later, and continued until the mid-1980s.

Everyman Theatre

Stories exchanged between staff and performers have long reigned through the years about the ghosts that inhabit the Victorian auditorium on Regent Street. In particular, the sound of unexplained music has been heard emanating from various locations, and eerie figures have been seen taking refuge in the upper seating levels.

Playhouse Theatre

Another show hall that is potentially haunted, particularly by the rumoured apparition of a young figure sitting on the edge of the stage, legs dangling. Perhaps this could be a bather, dipping their toes into what would have once been a swimming pool full of water? The theatre is on the site of an old pool, which replaced the original Montpellier Baths in 1898.

Cheltenham Under Attack!

Wartime bombardment

Cheltenham provided a haven for many evacuees during the Second World War, but it didn't escape the horrors of war entirely. During the air raids on Cheltenham during the latter part of 1940, and again in 1942, thirty-one people lost their lives. Twenty-three of those deaths occurred during the night of the 11 December 1940, when around 2,000 incendiary devices and 100 high explosives carried by the German Luftwaffe rained down over homes and buildings. Eyewitness accounts spoke of the key sites that were hit, including the aircraft works of H.H. Martyn at Sunningdale on the Lansdown Industrial Estate, the railway line at Pilley Bridge in Leckhampton, the Black and White coach station, and the Honeybourne railway line – an explosion here destroyed half of Stoneville Street in the process.

Cheltenham Grammar School improvised as a makeshift shelter for the 600 people left homeless.

Bus Bomb Scare

What was intended to be a training exercise for Stagecoach Bus staff turned into a serious emergency and a full-scale evacuation of Cheltenham's lower High Street on 31 August 2007. A suspicious package, intended to demonstrate security procedures, was discovered by passengers after being left behind on an operational bus. Roads were blockaded while a controlled explosion of the package took place. The bus operator later apologised to the passengers affected, and to the police and public.

House Prices

The following ten streets are the most expensive in which to buy property in Cheltenham (within the Borough boundary, as at 30 September 2011), according to Zoopla.co.uk's 'Zed-Index', detailing the current average Zoopla Estimate of home values per street:

Charlton Park Gate: £1,690,030

Sandy Lane Road: £1,045,453

Stanley Road: £999,496

Ashley Road: £979,177

Bayshill Road: £972,466

Imperial Square: £941,421

Greenhills Road: £928,879

Balcarras Retreat: £913,180

Balcarras Gardens: £873,650

Birchley Road: £869,070

Favourite Scene

Least Favourite Scene

Festivals

Cheltenham Festival
Four days of prestigious National Hunt racing, held in March, where the best British and Irish thoroughbreds traditionally compete, watched by as many as 200,000 spectators. This meeting holds one of the most lucrative prize purses in horse racing, and is usually well attended by royalty and the famous.

Cheltenham Festival of the Performing Arts
Formerly the Cheltenham Competitive Festival, and the town's oldest, starting in 1926. Performances and judging, in dance, music, and drama and speech, happen annually at the Town Hall.

Wychwood Music Festival
Often thought of, and promoted as, a very family-friendly festival, which launched in 2005. It mainly features live music, from the indie, folk and world music scene, as well as comedy and workshops.

Regularly nominated for Best Family Festival at the UK Festival Awards.

Greenbelt Festival
Held at the Racecourse since 1999, Greenbelt has grown into a popular Christian music event. Annually attended by over 20,000 people over the August Bank Holiday, it showcases music performances, talks and discussions.

Folk Festival
The first festival in the calendar year to get underway in the town, it boasts the very best of the UK folk music world. The first was in 1996, after the organiser of the Cheltenham Folk Club proposed an event to the Town Hall 'to banish the winter blues'.

Cheltenham Festivals

The not-for-profit organisation that has been striving to make Cheltenham the festival capital of Britain, with the production of four events; a study suggests that they have generated around £5.2 million worth of business for the local economy. The 'Big Four' are...

Jazz – The first was in 1996 and has become well established, with venues dotted around the town, including the outdoor 'Budvar Stage' in Imperial Gardens. The *Guardian* newspaper has called it 'one of the UK's classiest and most eclectic jazz festivals'.

Science – One of the newest to the collective, starting in 2002, it features the 'Discover Zone', which fills Cheltenham Town Hall with interactive learning experiences, as well as many talks and demonstrations.

Music – Featuring a programme of mainly classical music, and entertaining since its inception in 1945. Cheltenham Town Hall and Pittville Pump Room are the two main venues.

Literature – The oldest literature festival in the world, it makes great use of Cheltenham's central squares, featuring its entertainment in large marquees in Imperial and Montpellier Gardens. During a recent festival, one in five businesses in the town said they saw turnover rise by more than 10 per cent.

Royalty

King George III

The first significant royal to embrace Cheltenham life. Following long-term mental illness, and on the advice of his physicians, the King, together with Queen Charlotte, arrived in Cheltenham to recuperate and, most importantly, to take the spa waters (with the hope that an improvement in his health would occur). He stayed in Bayshill House (now Sidney Lodge, belonging to the Cheltenham Ladies' College), the home of one of his waiting staff, Lord Fauconberg. After sampling the waters every morning, the King would spend the rest of the day strolling around town with the royal party, sometimes visiting and conversing with local farmers, and even regularly attending performances at the town's theatre. It was this five-week period of residency that made Cheltenham the centre for high-society living.

Zara Phillips

The contemporary royal has lived in Cheltenham since April 2009, with her husband, Rugby Union player Mike Tindall, in a £1 million town house. They announced their engagement with photographs taken in the house's grounds in December 2010. The Queen's granddaughter is a regular fixture in the crowd at the Cheltenham Festival, where her dress sense is regularly admired by the press. In sport, equestrianism is Phillips' main passion, but she has also represented the Cheltenham Ladies' College in hockey.

Actors

Richard O'Brien

The actor and writer; he is best known for penning cult musical *The Rocky Horror Show*, and for presenting the innovative Channel 4 adventure game show *The Crystal Maze*. O'Brien was born Richard Timothy Smith in Cheltenham in 1951, but spent nine years of his youth in New Zealand.

Mark Lester

Fame came after landing the title role in the 1968 musical film *Oliver!*. Further film and television work followed before he retired from acting, at the age of nineteen, to train in alternative medicine. Lester lives in Cheltenham, where he practices as a fully qualified osteopath and acupuncturist at his business, the Carlton Clinic, established in 1993.

He recently returned to acting in 2011, playing King Harold in the film *1066*.

Sir Ralph Richardson

His work on the stage and big screen is much revered, including roles in *The Fallen Idol*, *The Sound Barrier* and, later, Terry Gilliam's *Time Bandits*. Richardson was born in Cheltenham, where his father was an art master at Cheltenham Ladies' College, but moved away at a young age when his parents separated. He launched the very first Cheltenham Literature Festival in 1949.

Robert Hardy

One of Britain's best-loved actors, appearing in *All Creatures Great And Small*, *Winston Churchill: The Wilderness Years*, and the *Harry Potter* film series. Hardy was born in Cheltenham, the son of a headmaster at Cheltenham College.

Martin Jarvis

A memorable face from the BBC television series *The Forsyte Saga*, and from stage roles in the West End, Jarvis is also a leading radio actor, director and producer. He was born in Cheltenham in 1941.

Sportspeople

Fred Archer
A Victorian jockey, described as 'the best all-round jockey that the Turf has ever seen' by the National Horseracing Museum. He trained in Prestbury, where his father was landlord of the Kings Arms pub. Archer rode his first winner at the age of twelve, and eventually achieved over 2,700 successes, spending thirteen consecutive years as Champion Jockey. He was unstoppable – until, suffering from a bout of depression, he committed suicide at the age of just twenty-nine.

Eddie 'The Eagle' Edwards
The Cheltenham plasterer who became famous for finishing last in his ski jump events at the 1988 Olympics in Calgary, despite being the UK's leader in the sport at the time. His failure became his success story, with worldwide fame from subsequent television and public appearances.

Zac Purchase
A world-class rower, and the winner of many Olympic and World Championship gold medals. Purchase was born in Cheltenham in 1986. He spent time as a rowing coach at Cheltenham College, and trained at their Boat Club in preparation for the Beijing Olympics in 2008.

Nigel Starmer-Smith
Former England rugby union scrum-half who also played for the Barbarians and, domestically, for Harlequins; he then became the face of BBC television's rugby union coverage in *Rugby Special*. Starmer-Smith also turned to print, and became the editor of *Rugby World*, the world's biggest-selling rugby magazine. He was born in Cheltenham on Christmas Day in 1944.

Fred Archer

Popular Music Heritage

Brian Jones

The founding member of the Rolling Stones, Jones was born in the Park Nursing Home on 28 February 1942. His first home was at 'Rosemead', an Edwardian red-brick house at No. 17 Eldorado Road, and later lived at No. 335 Hatherley Road. Jones attended Dean Close Junior School, and then Cheltenham Grammar School. He didn't shy away from the Cheltenham social scene, regularly hanging out at the Waikiki Club in Montpellier, and also at a jazz club in the converted basement of the home of Jane Filby, at No. 38 Priory Street. Jones' funeral took place at St Mary's parish church in July 1969. He was buried at the town's cemetery in a grand silver and bronze casket, commissioned by folk-rock hero and close friend Bob Dylan. The grave is almost always adorned with flowers and tributes.

'Heartache Avenue'

The 7in single front cover to this 1983 UK top ten single hit for The Maisonettes shows an image of the band relaxing at tables and chairs in Imperial Gardens.

'Beatlemania!'

This famous phrase can be attributed to a Fab Four concert at the Odeon Cinema on Winchcombe Street at 8 o'clock on the evening of the 1 November 1963. A headline in the Daily Mirror the following morning screamed 'Beatlemania! It's happening everywhere… even in sedate Cheltenham'. It's widely believed to be the first time that the term was used in print: shortly afterwards, everybody was saying it!

The Blue Moon

A venue that inhabited the upper floors of 170 High Street and was opened on 17 July 1965 by promoters Eddie Norman and Bill Reid. Previously it had been a hangout called the Egg and Bacon, and then a dancehall known as the SPA Lounge. During the second half of the 1960s, The Blue Moon became a mecca for the young and hip about town, with appearances by many big names including the Small Faces, The Drifters, Cream and The Who. One well-known gig featured Jimi Hendrix, who stepped on to the corner stage on 11 February 1967. It has been recently operating as The Night Owl.

Cheltenham has produced many other musicians:

Ian Dench, a musician with EMF, who scored a UK top three single hit with 'Unbelievable'.

Rob Fisher, one half of the 1980s band Climie Fisher, whose biggest hits were 'Love Changes (Everything)', and 'Rise To The Occasion'.

Jaz Coleman, the frontman for the rock band Killing Joke: they achieved moderate UK chart success during the mid 1980s. Coleman also became a composer of film scores and classical music.

Würzel, the guitarist with the heavy metal band Motörhead. Mainstream success came with the single 'Ace Of Spades'.

BLUE MOON

170 HIGH STREET, CHELTENHAM

Eddie Norman and Bill Reid

**SATURDAY, 11TH FEBRUARY 1967
7.30.-11.30**

HEY JOE - TOP TEN HIT

JIMI HENDRIX
EXPERIENCE

DISCOTHEQUE FRIDAY AND SUNDAY
FEATURING FRANKIE AND ROCKY
YOUR D.J.'S AND THE MOON GO-GO GIRLS

NEXT SATURDAY - THE ACTION

Coming Soon - GENO WASHINGTON

Sports Clubs & Associations

The town's premier football club is Cheltenham Town Football Club, playing in Football League Two, as of the 2011/2012 season. Founded in 1887, their nickname is 'The Robins', and home games are played at the Abbey Business Stadium on Whaddon Road.

Key dates:
1887: Club founded.

1935: Joined Southern League.

1985: Promoted to the Alliance Premier League (now Conference National).

1996: Appointment of Steve Cotterill as manager, 'The Robins' most successful.

1997-1998: FA Trophy winners.

1999: Full league status gained for the first time.

2002: Most successful run in the FA Cup, reaching the fifth round with an away tie against West Bromwich Albion. They lose 1-0.

2006: Promoted to Football League One after play-offs, under manager John Ward. Highest league position achieved.

Statistics (as at 30 September 2011):
Biggest win: 12-0 versus Chippenham Rovers, FA Cup third qualifying round, 2 November 1935.

Biggest defeat: 1-10 versus Merthyr Tydfil, Southern League, 8 March 1952.

Highest transfer: £400,000 for Steven Gillespie, sold to Colchester United in June 2008.

Most appearances: Roger Thorndale, who appeared 702 times between 1958 and 1976.

CHELTENHAM
TOWN FC

The headquarters of the **Croquet Association**, the national governing body for the sport in England, Wales and Northern Ireland, is on Old Bath Road. It was formed in 1897, and its patron is HM Queen Elizabeth II.

It moved to its current base in 2002, after a long association with The Hurlingham Club in London. In 2008, the Association presented John Prescott, the former Deputy Prime Minister, with a mallet as a gift in thanks for giving the game a boost in publicity. This followed his derision in the press over published photographs of Mr Prescott playing croquet in the garden of his home two years previously.

It is also the home of the **Cheltenham Croquet Club**, the largest of its kind in size in the country, with eleven lawns in total. It's also one of the oldest, founded in 1869, and originally established in Montpellier. The club hosts the majority of the game's national competitions, and also hosted the World Croquet Championships in 2005.

On Location

Cheltenham has been frequently used as a location for films and television programmes. Here are some of them...

Butterflies
The BBC sitcom about the lives of the Parkinson family. Several scenes were filmed in Hatherley Park, where Wendy Craig's character, Ria, would retire to for some contemplation over her unsatisfying suburban life. Exterior views of the family house were captured in nearby Bournside Road. Much more of the town featured, including scenes shot in Montpellier and the High Street.

The Whistle Blower
This British spy thriller, starring Michael Caine and Nigel Havers, centred its storyline on GCHQ, and showed parts of Montpellier, the railway station and Lansdown Place.

if....
Most of the scenes to Lindsay Anderson's satirical film portrayal of rebellious school life were filmed at Cheltenham College, where Anderson himself is an alumnus. Other scenes featured the now-demolished St John's church on Albion Street.

The television drama **Pride and Prejudice** featured Cheltenham Town Hall in a ballroom scene.

The Rise and Fall of Reginald Perrin with Leonard Rossiter saw some filming in Eldorado Road.

The television drama of **Vanity Fair** included the Pittville Pump Room and the Town Hall.

Ronnie Barker's comedy **Clarence** had a glimpse of Lansdown Terrace.

The House of Eliott, following a 1920s dressmaking business, featured scenes of Pittville Park and Pump Room, and also Regent Street and Ormond Place.

The Lost Railway

By the 1960s, mainly due to 'The Reshaping of British Railways' by Doctor Beeching – or the 'Beeching Axe' – Cheltenham's railway network had been severely cut. At the end of the decade, just one, at Lansdown, remained. Here are the casualties...

Cheltenham Spa St James – A terminus, only a stone's throw away from the town centre, closed to passenger traffic on 3 January 1966, with services diverted to Cheltenham's Lansdown. St James House and a supermarket now sit on the site at St James' Square.

Cheltenham Spa Malvern Road – Originally sited to the west of the Cheltenham Ladies' College Recreation Ground. It closed on 3 January 1966.

Cheltenham South and Leckhampton – The station from where the Banbury and Cheltenham Direct Railway truly began. Operational until 15 October 1962. It was positioned just to the east of where the Leckhampton Place apartment complex now stands, on Old Station Drive.

Charlton Kings – Once the next stop following Leckhampton, and also closed on 15 October 1962. The site is now occupied by the headquarters of the Chelsea Building Society.

Cheltenham High Street – Served north-west Cheltenham at the Tewkesbury Road bridge, north of the station at Lansdown. Closed 1 July 1910, after nearly forty-eight years.

Cheltenham High Street Halt – An unstaffed station open for just nine years, as part of the Honeybourne Line, it was located between the dead-end of Stoneville Street and the lower High Street. It closed in 1917 during the First World War, for economic reasons, and never re-opened.

There is a station at Cheltenham Racecourse, once used for passenger services, which remained partly operational until 1976, when it closed following a nearby derailment. It opened again in 2003, as part of the Gloucestershire Warwickshire heritage railway.

Statues & Monuments

Neptune's Fountain
At the south end of the Long Gardens, the god of water holds his trident aloft, while being showered in water taken from the River Chelt. Designed by Joseph Hall and constructed by R.L. Boulton and Sons in 1893.

Edward Wilson
Close to Neptune's Fountain is this memorial to the Cheltenham explorer. Another project undertaken by R.L. Boulton, it was unveiled in 1914.

Boer War Memorial
At the opposite end to Wilson stands a statue dedicated to those who lost their lives in combat in the South African conflict. It is another R.L. Boulton creation.

The Minotaur and the Hare
This striking image always attracts attention. It was sculpted by Sophie Ryder in 1995 for an exhibition at the Art Gallery & Museum, before being purchased for the town and placed in the pedestrianised area of the Promenade.

Gustav Holst Memorial Fountain
The first public dedication to the Cheltenham composer. Sculpted by Anthony Stones and unveiled in Imperial Gardens in 2008.

Imperial Fountain
A dainty figure hidden away at the east end of the Broadwalk, to the south of Imperial Gardens. Said to have been captured, following an Italian robbery, and sold to a Cheltenham solicitor.

Edward VII
Once a drinking fountain for horses with carriages, this figure sits at the south end of Montpellier Walk, and shows the monarch comforting a young child.

William IV
Erected in 1833 to commemorate the King's coronation. Found on the east side of Montpellier Gardens.

117

Promenade & St Mary's Church
Then & Now

The Future

The **North Place and Portland Street development scheme** is hoping to revamp what was once the site of the Black and White coach station, but more recently has provided parking for numerous vehicles, lying just north of the centre of town.

Cheltenham Borough Council detail an ambitious plan to create a hotel, food store, a public square, homes and affordable housing. The proposal of developer Auger Buchler has been earmarked as the leading scheme. The project is seen as a way of connecting the Promenade with the area of Pittville. As of the autumn of 2011, so far, detailed plans and drawings have been presented.

Essential Cheltenham

Take a panoramic view of Cheltenham from the top of Leckhampton Hill. ☐

Taste the spa waters at Pittville Pump Room. ☐

Marvel at the immense floral beauty of the Long Gardens and Imperial Gardens. ☐

Go shopping on the 'Prom'. ☐

Travel through time at Cheltenham Art Gallery & Museum. ☐

Seek refreshments in Montpellier's cafés and bars. ☐

Back a winner at the races at Cheltenham Racecourse. ☐

Row a boat across Pittville Lake. ☐

Visit one of Cheltenham's many festivals. ☐

Catch a show at the Everyman or Playhouse Theatre. ☐

Image Captions & Credits

Page:

2. 'Welcome' sign at the junction of Leckhampton Hill and Daisybank Road

3. Cheltenham's Coat of Arms (courtesy of Cheltenham Borough Council)

7. The Municipal Offices and Long Gardens

9. Location of Cheltenham on a map of the UK; the 'Centre Stone'

10. Approaching a fence at Cheltenham Racecourse (courtesy of MissChampers); Pittville Pump Room

11. The Cheltenham Ladies' College; Cheltenham Town Hall

13. The tiny passageway at the south of Normal Terrace; Kidnappers Lane

15. Café society in Montpellier (courtesy of Andrew Stawarz); at the entrance to the Battledown Estate

17. Awaiting departure at Royal Well bus station

19. The Everyman Theatre; Cheltenham College (courtesy of Adam Burt)

21. The Twin Towns signpost in Imperial Gardens; the River Thiou flowing through the city of Annecy (courtesy of Julien Bertrand); the 'Gänseliesel' or 'Goose Girl', Göttingen (courtesy of Abhijeet Rane)

23. Charman Road Shopping Strip, Cheltenham, Victoria, Australia (courtesy of iPostcodes.com.au); Cheltenham Badlands, Calendon, Ontario, Canada (courtesy of Ian Muttoo)

25. One of many black metal pigeons found on top of signposts, paying homage to the spa discovery; an illustration of King George III and Queen Charlotte at Cheltenham (courtesy of John Cassell's *Illustrated History of England*); the early years of the Cavendish House department store (courtesy of Cavendish House); the foundation stone of the Town Hall, which heralded the start of construction

27. A blanket of snow covering Imperial Gardens; summertime in Imperial Gardens (courtesy of Andy Miah); Bath Parade during the July 2007 floods (courtesy of Terry Jacombs, geograph.co.uk)

29. Ready to run at leisure@cheltenham (courtesy of Greg Chesters, leisure@cheltenham); The 'Wishing Fish' clock in the Regent Arcade Shopping Centre; tables set at Le Champignon Sauvage

31. The racecourse from Cleeve Hill (courtesy of Adrian Pingstone); many of the thousands of plants bedded around the town each year – these are in Imperial Gardens; packing up the stalls at the end of another Farmers' Market on the 'Prom' (courtesy of Pauline Eccles, geograph.co.uk)

33. The front façade of Christ Church on Malvern Road; the High Street populated with people

35. The Cheltenham–Paddington express, the 'Cheltenham Flyer', at Naas Crossing (courtesy of Ben Brooksbank, geograph.co.uk); Cavendish House (courtesy of Andrew Oakley); Sandford Parks Lido (courtesy of Iain Barton)

37. Illustration of William Cobbett (from *William Cobbett: A Biography*. By Edward Smith, 1878); George Jacob Holyoake (from *Life And Letters Of George Jacob Holyoake*. By Joseph McCabe, 1908)

39. Caricature of Captain (Thomas) Mayne Reid from *Vanity Fair*, March 8, 1873; Alfred Noyes (courtesy of United States Library Of Congress)

41. Air Chief Marshal Sir Arthur Harris, Commander in Chief of Royal Air Force Bomber Command; the explorer Edward Adrian Wilson

43. A statue of the composer Gustav Holst; the sweeping Regency terrace of Lansdown Crescent

45. A sign indicating the inner ring road (courtesy of Adrian Wallett); the daunting final fences on the home straight at Cheltenham Racecourse

47. A badge voicing support for the GCHQ workers belonging to Trade Unions (courtesy of Peter Alexander)

51. The Fathers 4 Justice protest at Buckingham Palace in 2004 (courtesy of E. Wayne Ross)

53. The elegant frontage of the Municipal Offices; the Quadrangle on the Promenade

55. The north aisle of St Mary's parish church, with its fine rose window in the North transept (courtesy of Brian Robert Marshall, geograph.co.uk); the imposing stature of Eagle Tower

57. An aerial view of the 'Doughnut', GCHQ's Benhall base (courtesy of GCHQ, Crown Copyright); the ill-fated Millennium Restaurant (courtesy of Helen Iwanczuk, geograph.co.uk)

59. The beauty of the Cheltenham caryatid

61. Exterior view of Sir Hugh Casson 1989 extension to the Cheltenham Art Gallery & Museum (courtesy of Cheltenham Art Gallery & Museum); 'The Old Man', the trade sign for a master chimney sweep, which formerly hung on the outside of 43 Sherborne Street in Fairview – found in the Art Gallery & Museum's 'Cheltenham History Galleries'

63. The exterior of the Holst Birthplace Museum; inside the Music Room at the Holst Birthplace Museum

64-5. The majesty of Cheltenham, as seen from the top of Leckhampton Hill

67. The feature fountain, on the West side of Sandford Park; the 'Weeping Beech' and cottage homes in Naunton Park

69. The bandstand in Montpellier Gardens; the central flood plain at Cox's Meadow

71. Mural depicting the escaping elephants on Albion Street in 1934; the 'Birds and Bunnies' at Pittville Park

73. The Dowty R391 Advanced Propeller System (courtesy of Jaro Nemček)

75. Thirlestaine Hall, the headquarters of Chelsea Building Society for thirty-eight years; the entrance to the UCAS headquarters

77. An illustration of James Agg-Gardner (courtesy of *Punch, Or The London Charivari*. Vol. 159. December 8th, 1920); one of the stained-glass windows dedicated to Charles de Ferrieres at St Peter's church in Leckhampton

79. Dr Edward Jenner; caricature entitled 'The Cow-Pock—or—the Wonderful Effects of the New Inoculation!' by British satirist James Gillray (courtesy of United States Library of Congress)

81. The legendary 'Dancing Ken Hanks' striking a pose in the High Street; town crier Ken Brightwell proclaiming the latest local crime figures on the Promenade (courtesy of Gloucestershire Constabulary)

83. The murderer Amelia Dyer; Tower Lodge, linked with the 'Torso Murder'

85. The churchyard of St Mary's church in Prestbury; the Prestbury House Hotel

87. 'St Anne's' on Pittville Circus Road